AMERICAN CITIES

LAS VEGAS

Lily Erlic

AV2
www.av2books.com

Step 1
Go to **www.av2books.com**

Step 2
Enter this unique code
ZTECWYXN9

Step 3
Explore your interactive eBook!

AV2 is optimized for use on any device

Your interactive eBook comes with...

Read

Audio
Listen to the entire book read aloud

Videos
Watch informative video clips

Weblinks
Gain additional information for research

Try This!
Complete activities and hands-on experiments

Key Words
Study vocabulary, and complete a matching word activity

Quizzes
Test your knowledge

Slideshows
View images and captions

View new titles and product videos at www.av2books.com

Contents

Get to Know Las Vegas

Las Vegas is the largest city in the state of Nevada. It is known for its hotels, shows, and fine dining. Many people come to see the city at night. This is when it comes alive with bright lights.

Map of Nevada

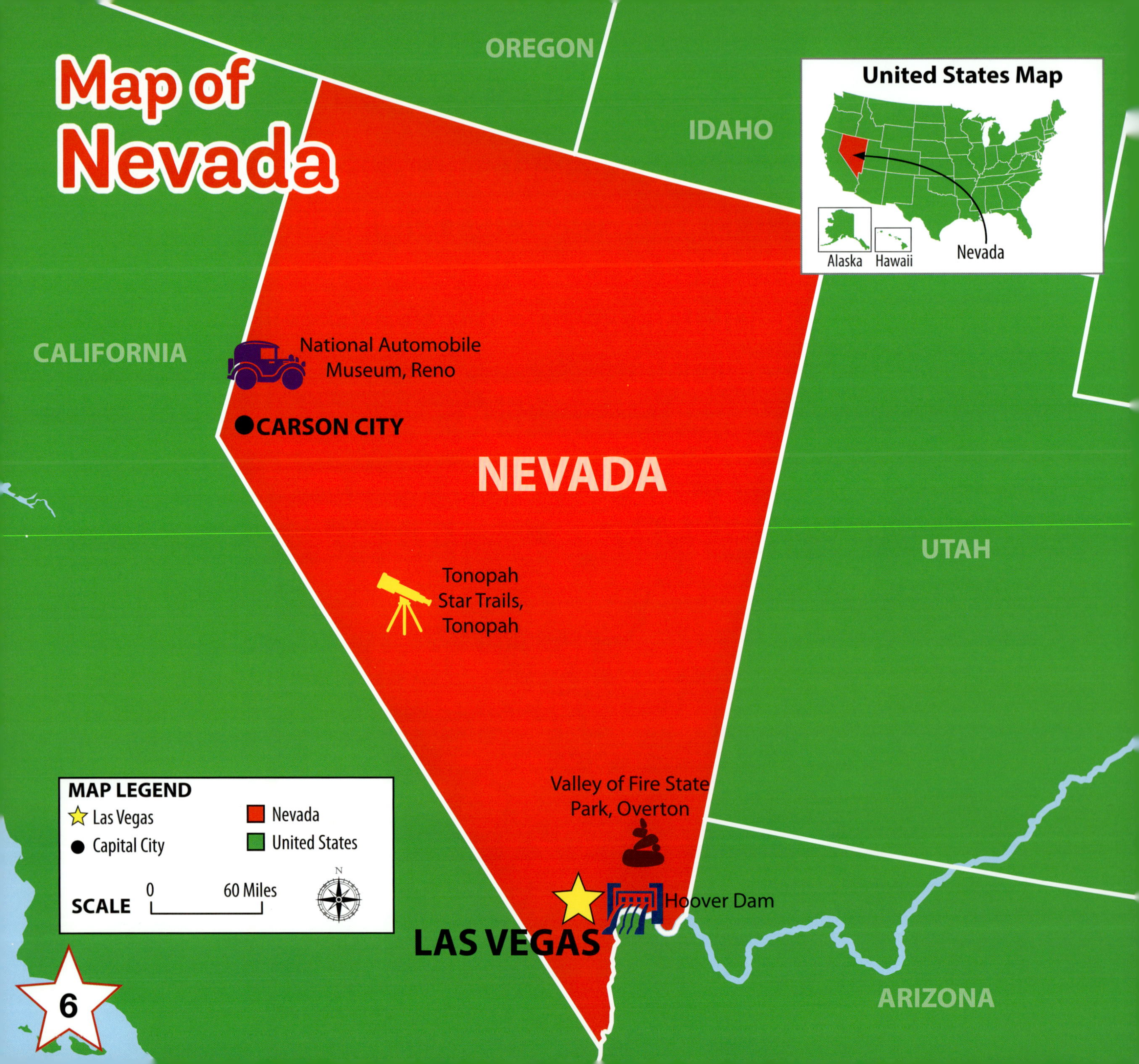

Where Is Las Vegas?

Las Vegas is in the southern part of Nevada. It is 432 miles southeast of Carson City, the state capital. You can get to Carson City from Las Vegas by taking the US-95 highway.

There are many other exciting places to visit in Nevada. You can use a road map to plan a trip. Which roads could you take from Las Vegas to get to these other places? How long might it take you to get to each place?

TRAVELING NEVADA
Las Vegas to Hoover Dam 37 miles
Las Vegas to Overton 63 miles
Las Vegas to Tonopah 211 miles
Las Vegas to Reno 438 miles

Climate

Las Vegas is very hot and dry in the summer. Heat waves can bring several days of high temperatures. The city does not get much rain.

Spring and fall are warm and sunny. Winter days are mild. Winter nights can be cold. Snow rarely falls on the city.

Las Vegas gets only about **4 inches** of rain each year.

VENETIAN

Population and Geography

Las Vegas is home to about 600,000 people. Another 1.4 million people live in the area around the city. Las Vegas is one of the fastest-growing cities in the United States.

Las Vegas sits within the Mojave Desert. The city is found at the bottom of a valley. Mountains rise on all sides of the city.

Many Peoples

Aboriginal Peoples were the first to live in the Las Vegas area. In 1829, Spanish explorers arrived. They were soon followed by American explorers. The first settlers arrived in 1855.

The settlers found the land too dry to grow crops. Many moved away. In 1905, a railroad began running through Nevada. One of its rest stops was Las Vegas. This brought new settlers to the area.

In **1900**, only **30 people** lived in Las Vegas.

1900 Blacksmith Shop
(replica)
Eagle Scout Project

Tourism

Visitors to Las Vegas often walk along the Las Vegas Strip. This street is where most of the city's big hotels are found. Many of the hotels have fun things for visitors to see and do. The Bellagio has an outdoor water show. Its fountains dance to music.

There are more than **1,000 fountains** in front of the Bellagio.

The High Roller is also found on the Strip. It is the world's tallest Ferris wheel. People who ride it get great views of the city.

Sports

Las Vegas has three major sports teams. The Vegas Golden Knights play hockey for the city. The Las Vegas Aces play basketball. The Las Vegas Raiders will begin playing football for the city in 2020.

Each team has a place to play its home games. The Golden Knights play at the T-Mobile Arena. The Aces play at the Mandalay Bay Events Center. The Raiders will play at Allegiant Stadium.

XA-VAR
viva
interjet
E3

Economy

Tourism is big business in Las Vegas. Every year, about 40 million people visit the city. They spend their money on hotels, food, and shows.

Most people come to Las Vegas by air. This has made McCarran International Airport one of the busiest airports in the country. In 2018, more than 49 million people came through this airport.

In **2018**, tourists spent about **$34.5 billion** in Las Vegas.

Las Vegas Timeline

10,000 years ago
Aboriginal Peoples live in the Las Vegas area.

1829
Spanish explorers arrive in the area.

1855
The area's first settlers arrive and build a fort.

1905
The town of Las Vegas is founded.

1911
Las Vegas becomes a city.

2005
Las Vegas celebrates its 100th birthday.

1998
The Bellagio opens. It is the world's most expensive hotel at the time.

2019
The first Las Vegas Pizza Festival is held.

Things to Do in Las Vegas

Stratosphere Tower
At 1,149 feet, this tower is the tallest structure in Las Vegas. Besides great views, it offers several thrill rides. Visitors can take the SkyJump off the tower or ride a giant seesaw.

Las Vegas Natural History Museum
Visitors to this museum can dig for fossils and see what is inside an Egyptian mummy. They can even view a 35-foot model of a dinosaur.

Shark Reef Aquarium

This aquarium is home to more than 2,000 sea creatures, such as sharks and sea turtles. Many are housed within the 1.3 million-gallon shipwreck tank.

Pinball Hall of Fame

The history of pinball is on display at this museum. It houses more than 200 pinball machines from the 1930s to present day.

Adventuredome Theme Park

This is one of the largest indoor amusement parks in the United States. It offers 25 rides, a miniature golf course, and a rock-climbing wall.

KEY WORDS

Research has shown that as much as 65 percent of all written material published in English is made up of 300 words. These 300 words cannot be taught using pictures or learned by sounding them out. They must be recognized by sight. This book contains 119 common sight words to help young readers improve their reading fluency and comprehension. This book also teaches young readers several important content words, such as proper nouns. These words are paired with pictures to aid in learning and improve understanding.

Page	Sight Words First Appearance
4	get, know, to
5	and, at, city, come, for, in, is, it, its, lights, many, night, of, people, see, shows, state, the, this, when, with
7	a, are, by, can, could, each, from, how, long, might, miles, other, part, places, take, there, these, use, where, which, you
8	about, be, days, does, high, much, not, on, only, very, year
11	all, another, around, found, home, live, mountains, one, sides
12	American, away, began, first, grow, land, moved, new, soon, stops, they, through, too, was, were
15	along, also, an, big, do, great, has, have, more, most, often, than, things, walk, water, who, world
16	begin, play, three, will
19	air, came, country, every, food, made, their
21	opens, time
22	even, feet, off, or, what
23	as, housed, sea, such

Page	Content Words First Appearance
4	Las Vegas
5	dining, hotels, Nevada
7	capital, Carson City, highway, map, roads, trip
8	climate, fall, heat waves, inches, rain, snow, spring, summer, temperatures
11	area, bottom, crops, geography, Mojave Desert, population, United States, valley
12	Aboriginal Peoples, explorers, railroad, settlers
15	Bellagio, Ferris wheel, fountains, High Roller, Las Vegas Strip, music, street, tourism, views, visitors
16	Allegiant Stadium, basketball, games, hockey, Las Vegas Aces, Las Vegas Raiders, Mandalay Bay Events Center, sports, teams, T-Mobile Arena, Vegas Golden Knights
19	business, economy, McCarran International Airport, money, tourists
20	fort, timeline, town
21	birthday, Las Vegas Pizza Festival
22	dinosaur, Egyptian mummy, fossils, Las Vegas Natural History Museum, model, rides, seesaw, SkyJump, Stratosphere Tower, structure
23	Adventuredome Theme Park, creatures, history, machines, miniature golf course, Pinball Hall of Fame, rock-climbing wall, sea turtles, Shark Reef Aquarium, tank

Published by AV2
350 5th Avenue, 59th Floor New York, NY 10118
Website: www.av2books.com

Library of Congress Cataloging-in-Publication Data
Names: Erlic, Lily, author.
Title: Las Vegas / Lily Erlic.
Description: New York, NY : AV2 by Weigl, [2021] | Series: American cities | Audience: Ages 6-9 | Audience: Grades 2-3 | Summary: "American Cities takes young readers on a tour of our capitals and major centers. Each book explores the geography, history, and people that give the featured city its distinctive flair."-- Provided by publisher.
Identifiers: LCCN 2019041021 (print) | LCCN 2019041022 (ebook) | ISBN 9781791115821 (library binding) | ISBN 9781791115838 (paperback) | ISBN 9781791115845 | ISBN 9781791115852
Subjects: LCSH: Las Vegas (Nev.)--History--Juvenile literature.
Classification: LCC F849.L35 E75 2021 (print) | LCC F849.L35 (ebook) | DDC 979.3/135--dc23
LC record available at https://lccn.loc.gov/2019041021
LC ebook record available at https://lccn.loc.gov/2019041022

Printed in Guangzhou, China
1 2 3 4 5 6 7 8 9 0 24 23 22 21 20

012020
100919

Project Coordinator: Heather Kissock Designer: Ana María Vidal

AV2 acknowledges Getty Images, Alamy, Newscom, Shutterstock, and iStock as the primary image suppliers for this title.